W9-BUE-858

year, more than 12,000 of these jointed toy bears had been shipped to the United States.

Capitalizing on the fame of Berryman's cartoon bear, advertisements heralded the arrival in stores of "Teddy's bear, imported directly from Germany." This advertising phrase caught on quickly as the demand for toy bears increased. Finally, the phrase was shortened to "teddy bear," a term that still refers to all stuffed toy bears.

while observing bear cubs at the Stuttgart Zoo.

Although Margarete was disappointed with her creation, Richard was delighted and arranged to introduce the new design at the Leipzig Trade Fair. Margarete's toy bear received a lukewarm reception among European buyers, but an American distributor bought 3,000 of them, and soon doubled his original order. By the end of the first

Contents

The
Quotable

TEDDY
BEAR

Introduction

On a brisk November morning in 1902, Theodore "Teddy" Roosevelt, the President of the United States, embarked on a hunting trip in Mississippi. He had gone south to settle a border dispute between Mississippi and Louisiana, and to enjoy a bit of relaxation with his friends and fellow hunters. This was bear country, but on that day, none could be found.

After lunch, word reached the President's party that a bear had been sighted. They set out with excitement. What they found was a tired old bear tied to a tree. Offended, the President refused to shoot the bear, claiming that it would be unsportsmanlike and that his children would never forgive him.

Back East, political cartoonist Clifford Berryman of the *Washington Post* heard of the President's

The
Quotable

TEDDY
BEAR

RUNNING PRESS
PHILADELPHIA · LONDON

Canadian representatives: General Publishing Co., Ltd.,
30 Lesmill Road, Don Mills, Ontario M3B 2T6.

Library of Congress Cataloging-in-Publication Number 94–73886

ISBN 1-56138-517-4

This book may be ordered by mail from the publisher. Please add
$1.00 for postage and handling. *But try your bookstore first!*

Running Press Book Publishers
125 South Twenty-second Street
Philadelphia, Pennsylvania 19103–4399

Teddies go everywhere and do everything. There is not a corner of the globe that they have not penetrated, if not with children then with adults. Their appeal is universal and to all ages. They have gone into battle on guns, tanks and in haversacks; saved lives by intercepting bullets . . . are used extensively in advertising campaigns; collected encounter. The following day Berryman's cartoon appeared depicting the President befriending a small, shivering bear. Its title, "Drawing the Line in Mississippi," referred to both the hunting incident and the border dispute. The cartoon delighted readers across the country and softened the otherwise stern image of the President.

Berryman continued to use the little bear cub in all of his Roosevelt cartoons, forever linking him to the President. The cub, which often appeared as a sideline commentator in the cartoons, came to be known as "Teddy's bear."

Meanwhile, across the Atlantic Ocean in Giengen, Germany, a wheelchair-bound toymaker named Margarete Steiff was busy creating a stuffed toy bear. She based her design on the sketches her nephew Richard, an art student, had made

Myths about the teddy bear's creation abound. Among the legends is the story of Morris and Rose Michtom, who founded the Ideal Toy Company. Ideal marketed a stuffed toy bear similar to Steiff's not long after Roosevelt's well-known hunting encounter. According to the tale, the couple wrote to the President, asking permission to call their bears "Teddy."

Roosevelt was said to have replied that they could, but that he saw no reason why his name might have any appeal. While there is no evidence to support this story—no copies of either letter were ever found—it is still a charming tale.

From Roosevelt's bear, Berryman's cartoon, and Steiff's toy came the teddy bear. Since its introduction in 1903, the teddy bear has remained one of the most popular toys of all time, cherished by girls and boys alike. This book, a collection of quotes from arctophiles (bear lovers) of all ages, captures teddy's enduring appeal. Inspired by an act of compassion, the teddy bear continues to befriend all in the name of love.

—*Ted Menten*

BEST
Companions

There is no need to tell you how special the teddy bear is. He has been around for over eighty years and has never slipped down the popularity stakes. Within five years of birth, almost every child in the United States had his or her own teddy to love. At first, he was seen as filling a need for a boys' toy, where girls had dolls. But boys and girls took to him equally, and maintained their affection well into adulthood.

Josa Keyes
English fashion
& feature writer

Teddy bears . . .
seem to possess an
endearing quality of
listening without
judging.

Bo Niles
American writer
& editor

No other animal has enjoyed anything like the enduring popularity of the teddy bear, nor have they given rise to quite so many stories: tales of love and kindness, steadfastness, honour and bravery, good manners and thought for others. In short, all the qualities which, deep down, we know to be good and wish we had ourselves.

Michael Bond
English writer

Bears make life
more bearable. They
are remarkable com-
pany when one
is alone.

Nesta Wynn Ellis
English teddy bear
collector

by film stars, ballerinas and actresses; used as mascots and talismans; had endless books, songs and verses written about them; are taken to hospitals; are indeed part of our everyday life. . . .

Margaret Hutchings
English teddy bear
artist & writer

[Teddy] bears are so versatile;
they can be traveling companions,
shoulders to cry on . . . alter egos,
especially appealing decorations,
playthings, bedfellows—goodness,
what other creatures (flesh-and-
blood or fibre-filled) can play
so many varied roles?!

Victoria Marsden
English teddy bear artist

A teddy bear can be soft and nice to hug, the kind of bear that is required to be able safely to fall asleep. But a teddy bear can also be so much else—anything from an astronaut or a commando to an explorer out on an adventure, or quite simply an ordinary citizen in an advanced bear society.

Erik Ronne
Swedish writer

Teddy bears are soothing creatures, attentive and sensitive to the
owner's moods. Protective feelings
expressed toward the teddy bears
might be extended toward
fellow humans.

Margaret Fox Mandel
American teddy bear
collector & writer

A teddy bear's
virtue is that he can-
not love himself . . .
only others.

Ted Menten
American teddy bear
artist & writer

Even though
there's a rip in your
teddy bear, his love
will not fall out.

Eve Frances Gigliotti
& Elaine Claire Gigliotti
American writers

. . . *of all* the beautiful and sentimental examples of human love, creativity and craft, the teddy bear is my favorite.

Linda Mullins
American writer

For a teddy bear . . . to be an art object, it must rise above the ordinary, and I believe this is best done through creating an emotive quality in its face—something about the eyes—which reaches out and touches the viewer's soul.

Carol-Lynn Rössel Waugh
Teddy bear artist & writer

The mystique lies
in the faces of the
bears themselves.

Peter Bull
English writer

His fur is badly worn, there is
a big bald spot on the back of his
head, and his joints are very weak.
Should I? . . . . Turning to go,
I see how disappointed the bear
is. "Please," he says, "I won't
be any trouble."

Jama Kim Rattigan
American teddy bear
collector & writer

Bears should make you feel good. If a bear makes me smile, that is grand. If he or she makes me laugh out loud, he or she will come home with me.

Rosemary Volpp
Teddy bear collector

Our prescription for the good life is a chicken in every pot, a car in every garage, and a teddy bear in every heart.

Gail Raznov
American scholar

Best-behaved

BEARS

The teddy bear: Heart-grabbing mix of trust and doubt ineffable. . . . Little soft thing sent forth to make his simple way in a world so slow to hug.

Jeanne Wylie Torosian
American writer

Teddy bears are innocent, clean-living, upstanding citizens.

Anonymous

For Republican conventions, and meetings associated with Roosevelt, the "Teddy Bear" became the standard decoration, more in evidence than the eagle, and only less usual than the Stars and Stripes.

Mark Sullivan
American writer

Bears and dolls are so very different. Dolls are always lady-like in their manners, but there is no counting on the actions of bears.

Playthings *magazine*

Teddy bears are remarkably adaptable. How many other life forms can survive being kicked out of bed in the middle of the night, thrown in the washing machine with the dirty socks, and fed a constant diet of Crayolas and Play-Doh?

Sarah McClellan
American writer

If there's one
thing a bear loves
more than sweets,
it's more sweets.

Walt Morey
American writer

It's pleasant for a bear to come home to the warmth of a fire, take a dollop of honey, talk to a friend, read the *Daily Bear News*, and finally creep under the quilt and sleep soundly all night.

Barbara Werkmaster,
Eva-Lena Bengsston,
& Per Peterson
Swedish writers

Teddy bears like to go on morning picnics in the summertime, so they can enjoy the sunshine before it is too hot for their furry selves.

Abigail Darling
American writer

When the eminent Marlon Perkins of the St. Louis Zoo and the television program *The Wild Kingdom* was asked what the single most pop- ular animal was, he replied: "The bears."

Patricia N. Schoonmaker
American writer
& collector

If I ask myself what kind of animal I'd like to come back as, I would say a bear. They are thoughtful, endearing creatures.

Jean-Charles de Castelbajac
French designer

Furry Bear

If I were a bear,
    And a big bear too,
I shouldn't much care
    If it froze or snew;
I shouldn't much mind
    If it snowed or friz—
I'd be all fur-lined
    With a coat like his!
For I'd have fur boots and a
    brown fur wrap,

And brown fur knickers and a big
    fur cap.
I'd have a fur muffle-ruff to cover
    my jaws,
And brown fur mittens on my
    big brown paws,
With a big brown furry-down
    up to my head,
I'd sleep all the winter in a
    big fur bed.

A.A. Milne
English writer

It is most offensive to the
kindly bears who've adopted us
when we thoughtlessly blurt out
some comment about "real" bears,
or "alive" bears, as if our very real
and lively bear friends weren't.

Alla Bozarth-Campbell
American cleric & writer

Best-loved
BEARS

The best authors have created unique characters for their furry heroes. Teddy might be full of stuffing, but he knows what is right and always holds onto his moral sense, even when there is dreadful (usually edible) temptation.

Josa Keyes
English fashion
& feature writer

There, sitting on his ample ginger bottom behind a blackberry bush, was Teddy, one paw clasped across his chest and the claws of his other paw stuffed into his mouth, singing to himself.

Gerald Durrell
English writer

That . . . was Lord Sebastian
Flyte. A *most* amusing young gen-
tleman. . . . What do you suppose
Lord Sebastian wanted? A hair
brush for his Teddy-bear; it had to
have very stiff bristles, *not*, Lord
Sebastian said, to brush him with,
but to threaten him with a
spanking when he was sulky.

He bought a very nice one with
an ivory back and he's having
"Aloysius" engraved on it—that's
the bear's name.

Evelyn Waugh
English writer

Here is Edward Bear, coming downstairs now, bump, bump, on the back of his head, behind Christopher Robin. It is, as far as he knows, the only way of coming downstairs, but sometimes he feels that there really is another way, if only he could stop bumping for a moment and think of it. And then,

he feels that perhaps there isn't.
Anyhow, here he is at the bottom,
and ready to be introduced to
you. Winnie-the-Pooh.

A.A. Milne
English writer

I'm really Edward George
    St. Clare,
Aubrey Adolphus de la Bear
Son and heir of the Baron Bear
But you may call me Teddy Bear.
So please me, squeeze me,
    I don't care.

Anonymous

Paddington nodded thoughtfully as he peered out of the car window. He had enjoyed his holiday in France no end, but it *was* nice knowing that each day brought something new.

"That's the best of being a bear," said Mrs. Bird. "Things happen to bears."

Michael Bond
English writer

Does Tussah Bear have a philosophy on life? I think so. It's something like, "Love hard and only one person; stay with them as long as they want you, and never leave them alone. Be prepared to venture out into the world with them, and never be afraid."

Jennifer Paulson
American writer

This tiny teddy's stitched nose long ago gave way to embraces, as did his red felt tongue; a whisper of crimson thread marks the spot. . . . His plush may be loved-off, but his slightly askew tarnished black metal eyes still seem wise.

Carol-Lynn Rössel Waugh
Teddy bear artist & writer

from
Summoned by Bells

I heard the church bells hollowing
    out the sky,
Deep beyond deep, like never-
    ending stars,
And turned to Archibald, my safe
    old bear,
Whose woollen eyes looked sad or
    glad at me,

Whose half-moon ears received
    my confidence,
Who made me laugh, who never
    let me down.
I used to wait for hours to see
    him move,
Convinced that he could breathe.

John Betjeman
English poet

No one would claim that he is beautiful, and yet everyone is captivated by his charm.

Yvonne Thalheim
American Writer

The most beautiful toy is worn and frazzled with love. It has shared confidences and has been dragged, wagged, hugged, squeezed, and slept with over the years. What memories that soft little body must hold. It's a good friend, becoming more treasured with the passing of time.

Kay Duggins
American writer

Anyone who has looked
a teddy bear in the face will
recognize the friendly
twinkle in his knowing look.

Harold Nadolny
American writer

To go to bed at
night I like panda
my little bear
because he keeps
me nice and warm[.]
We talk secretly.

Natalie Price
8-year-old
English student

Go to sleep, my Teddy Bear,
Close your little button eyes,
And let me smooth your hair.
It feels so soft and silky that,
I'd love to cuddle down by you,
So, Go to sleep, my darling
Teddy Bear.

Lullaby

FRIENDS
Forever

Family-owned and worn bears are records of loving hearts. They are as much a part of treasured family history as china, jewelry, or silver.

Beverly Matteson Port
American teddy bear
artist & collector

If you love bears,
you love children.

Linda Mullins
American writer

Surely, never has a toy so caught the imagination of children as the teddy bear. "Walking upright" as they do, yet not a human but a fluffy, lazy, lumbering, caricature of a well-loved animal, he somehow fills their every need.

Margaret Hutchings
English teddy bear
artist & writer

Long before I grew up, my teddy bear taught me what love really meant—being there when you're needed.

Jim Nelson
American writer

There is a personal relationship with teddy bears that never releases its grip. Who can forget a real friend, perhaps the only friend who really understood? The only one who could see a polar bear on the lawn or a witch in the old house in the woods? Or the only

one who hugged you hard when
the ghost appeared at the
bedroom window?

*Barbara Werkmaster,
Eva-Lena Bengsston,
& Per Peterson
Swedish writers*

In our childhood, teddy bears are warm companions—good listeners, never critical, always reassuring. They are bear-shaped security blankets, huggable enough to fold in our arms, a perfect fit for our laps.

Peggy & Alan Bialosky
American writers & editors

Teddy bears and Christmas just seem to go together. Perhaps it is because the holidays inspire the same feelings as teddies—of warmth, love, happiness and security. The furry faces are a constant reminder of the childlike joy that lies within each of us, just waiting to be awakened.

Anonymous

When Mama took my teddy away, she said it was time for me to grow up. Silly mother, not to know how wise a bear can be!

William Sternman
American writer

There are toys
for all ages

French proverb

You really don't
have to be young to
find a friend in a
teddy bear.

Rachel Newman
American writer
& editor

Possession of a
teddy bear after a
certain age is a very
private matter
indeed.

Peter Bull
English writer

Nobody can talk
about teddy bears
around me and get
away with it. . . .

George Steinbrenner
American baseball
executive

Does maturity mean abandoning our beloved teddy bears, and truest childhood friends, or does it mean being strong enough to proudly proclaim our devotion to them?

Ted Menten
American teddy bear
artist & writer

It is astonishing, really, how many thoroughly mature, well-adjusted grown-ups harbor a teddy bear—which is perhaps *why* they are thoroughly mature and well-adjusted.

Joseph Lempa
American writer

For adults, teddy bears are symbols of nostalgia, sort of furry Peter Pans that allow a very small part of each of us to remain a child forever. Could anyone ask for a more devoted friend?

Peggy & Alan Bialosky
American writers & editors

Once a bear
has been loved
by a human being,
its expression is
forever marked.

Jama Kim Rattigan
American teddy bear
collector & writer

The brand-new teddy on my shelf will always be a stranger. But the tattered bear I hold so tight will be my friend forever.

Jean Vande Zande
American writer

Where is he now? I don't
know. He got lost in the shuffle
of what is called the growing-up
process, but he never stopped
following me, and sometimes
when I thoughtfully look back,

there he is, looking at me with
that surprised expression that
says, "Hi! How y' doing?"

Marcus Bach
American writer

My teddy! He
was filled out with
the stuff of dreams.

Heidi Mair
American writer

Acknowledgments

p. 64: "Furry Bear" from *Now We Are Six* by A. A. Milne. Illustrations by E. H. Shepard. Copyright © 1927 by E. P. Dutton, renewed © 1955 by A. A. Milne. Used by permission of Dutton Children's Books, a division of Penguin Books USA.

p. 82: From "Summoned by Bells" by John Betjeman. Used by permission of John Murray Publishers, Ltd.

This book has been bound using handcraft methods, and Smyth-sewn to ensure durability.

The dust jacket was designed by Toby Schmidt.
The interior was designed by Taffy.
The photographs are by Ulrike Schneiders,
provided by H. Armstrong Roberts, Inc.
The text was edited by
Tara Ann McFadden and Elizabeth Broadrup.
The photographs were researched by
Susan Oyama.
The text was set in Schneidler and Weiss
by Justin T. Scott.